# Billy
# the Bulldozer

Written and Illustrated by Read With You
Center for Excellence in STEAM Education

**Read With You**

Published by Read With You Publishing. Printed in the United States of America.

Read With You and associated logos are trademarks and/or registered trademarks of Read With You L.L.C.

ISBN-13: 979-8-88618-054-1

First Edition March 2022

*Boom!* *Smash!* *Crash!*
Here comes Billy.

Billy is a bulldozer.
He is big, yellow, and tough as nails.

See that pile of dirt?
*Smash!*
Billy makes it flat with his
track chains!

See those tall plants?
*Scoop*!
Billy lifts them with
his blade!

See those dead trees?
*Crunch*!
Billy slices them with
his ripper!

"Billy!" Farmer Percy calls.
"I need help!"

Oh, dear.
Farmer Percy's farm is a big mess.
How can Billy help?

*Crunch!  Crunch!*
Billy breaks the rocks with
his ripper.

Crunch
Crunch
Crunch

*Scoop!* *Drop!*
Billy moves the dirt with
his blade.

*Vroom! Vroom!*
Billy flattens soil with his track chains.

That's better!
Now, Farmer Percy can plant
flowers.

"Billy!" Builder Kylie calls.
"I need help!"

Oh, dear.
Kylie's old porch is a mess.
How can Billy help?

*Crunch! Crunch!*
Billy breaks the old porch
with his ripper.

*Scoop! Drop!*
Billy moves the boards with
his blade.

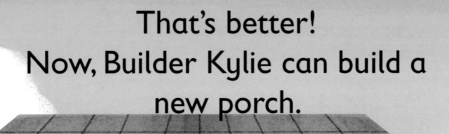

That's better!
Now, Builder Kylie can build a
new porch.

"I need help!" someone calls.
Who is that?!

Oh, dear.
Jessie is stuck behind these stones!
How can Billy help?

*Crunch!*
Billy breaks the stones
with his ripper.

*Scoop! Drop!*
Billy moves the stones
with his blade.

"Hop in!" Billy calls.
Billy carries Jessie in his cab.

Hooray! Jessie is home!
But, what's this?

**Break this, Billy!**

A wall? For Billy?
But, why?

Billy breaks the wall with his ripper.
He moves the bricks with his blade.

He revs his engine as he goes in.
What's this?

A flower bed?!
And a new garage!

# Learner's Guide

## Explore

**Practice 1: Questions**

Choose the correct answer.

1. Billy is a _____ .
   a. bulldozer
   b. tractor
   c. truck

2. Billy helps _____ .
   a. carry
   b. build
   c. deliver

Billy

3. Billy's track chains _____ dirt.
   a. rip
   b. flatten
   c. build

4. Billy's blade _____ stones.
   a. lifts
   b. rips
   c. flattens

Percy

5. Billy breaks things with his _____ .
   a. cab
   b. ripper
   c. blade

## Practice 2: Vocabulary

Look at the image of Billy below. Can you remember what each part is called? Label Billy with words from the word bank.

| Word Bank | | | |
|---|---|---|---|
| ripper | track chains | cab | blade |

#  Connect

- How do bulldozers help?

- What can a bulldozer do?

- Where might you find a bulldozer?

- Who usually drives a bulldozer?

- Would you like to drive a bulldozer?

#  Craft

**Project 1: Design**

In this book, Kylie and Percy build Billy a garage to say thank you. Imagine you are building a garage! Design it on a separate piece of paper. Color the garage door and the walls. Then, show it off to a buddy. Would they want to park a car in there?

# Project 2: Draw Billy

Let's get crafty! Find a separate sheet of paper and a pen. Copy the steps below to draw Billy the bulldozer.

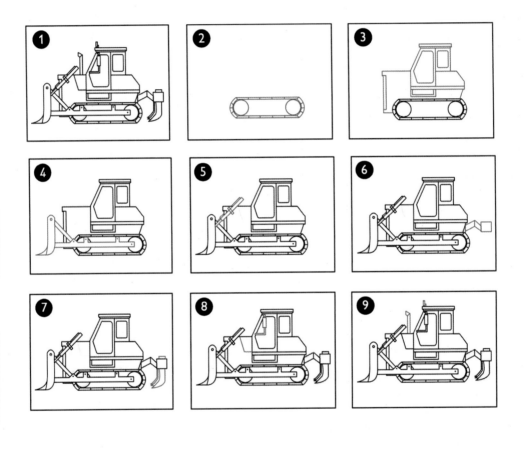

Made in the USA
Monee, IL
25 November 2022

18527549R00021